Do You Know?

HOW
DINOSAURS
LIVED

By
Michael Benton
Illustrated by
Jim Robins

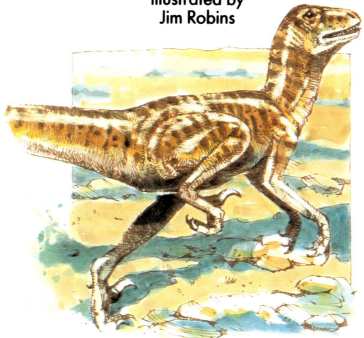

A Piccolo
Piper Book

Contents

The dinosaurs lived a very long time ago— before the first people appeared on the Earth.

There were hundreds of different kinds of dinosaurs. Many were much bigger than any other land animals that have ever existed. But others were no bigger than chickens.

Some dinosaurs walked on all fours; others on their hind legs. Some ate plants and others ate meat. There were dinosaurs with horns, spines, sharp claws, and big teeth, and some of them looked very strange.

Dinosaurs may seem like the dragons in fairy tales, but they were real animals which lived all over the Earth—and almost certainly they walked around just where you are sitting, reading this book.

Scientists have dug up hundreds of dinosaur skeletons, and they now know a lot about what dinosaurs looked like and how they lived. This book will tell you about some of the most interesting dinosaurs.

1 When Dinosaurs Ruled

The dinosaurs were on the Earth for over 150 million years, but they did not all live together at the same time. There were three different 'ages' in which dinosaurs lived.

The first group of dinosaurs lived 220 million years ago, in the Triassic period. These very early dinosaurs included lightly-built, fast-running kinds which ate meat (see above), and larger plant eaters which could feed high in the trees. The Triassic world was generally warm, and many areas were covered with deserts—even in Europe and North America. There was no grass at all, and the plants were mostly early kinds of pine tree as well as lower bushy plants and ferns.

The second age of dinosaurs was the Jurassic period (210—145 million years ago). A wide variety of dino-saurs lived near the end of the Jurassic

—some of them are shown in the centre picture. Many of them lived in lowland areas, where increasing amounts of rain made the conifer trees and tree ferns, the ferns and the various swamp plants grow thickly.

The third age of dinosaurs was the Cretaceous. The scene above shows the world about 75 million years ago. Some plant-eating dinosaurs carried horns or spikes to protect them from the ferocious meat eaters. By this time, evergreen trees and flowering plants had arrived.

By 65 million years ago, all the dinosaurs had disappeared.

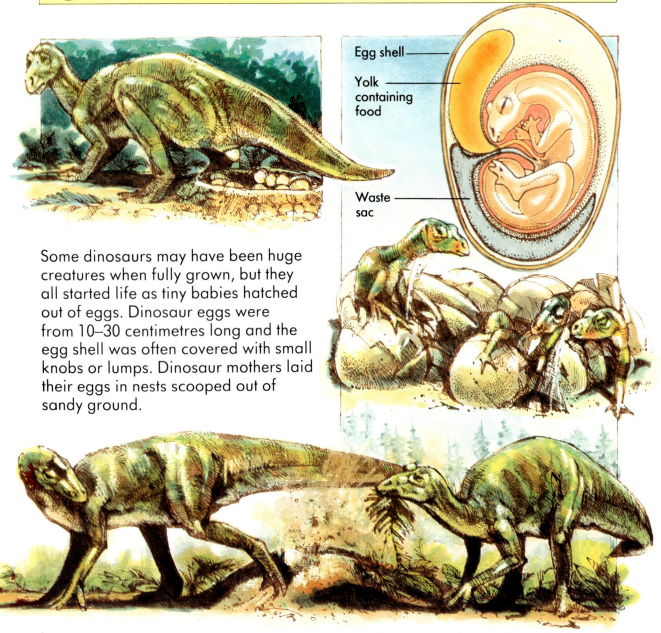

2 The Life Of A Dinosaur

Egg shell

Yolk containing food

Waste sac

Some dinosaurs may have been huge creatures when fully grown, but they all started life as tiny babies hatched out of eggs. Dinosaur eggs were from 10–30 centimetres long and the egg shell was often covered with small knobs or lumps. Dinosaur mothers laid their eggs in nests scooped out of sandy ground.

Dinosaur eggs and nests have been found in many parts of the world, but we know most about the eggs and nests of a dinosaur called *Maiasaura*.

  Maiasaura built a nest about 2 metres across and 0.75 metres deep—about the size of a large paddling pool. The mother laid from 20 to 25 eggs in the nest and then covered them over with sand and pieces of plants to keep them warm. The babies grew inside the eggs and then hatched out when they were about 0.5 metres long.

The baby dinosaurs were small and were probably in danger of being eaten by other animals. But the adults stayed to protect them, and may have fed them with plants.

At first, a young *Maiasaura* probably grew very quickly. A three-year-old would be twice the size of a one-year-old, and at four or five, *Maiasaura* was fully grown.

At the age of five or six, *Maiasaura* was an adult and was ready to be a mother or father itself. The new mother may have gone back to lay its eggs where it was born.

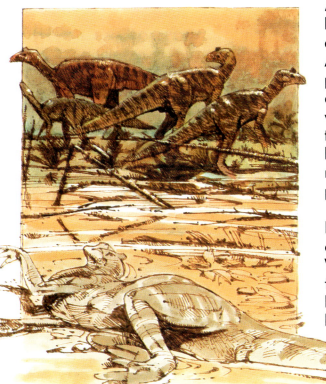

Maiasaura was a plant eater and we believe that it lived in large herds, just as antelope do today on the plains of Africa. There must have been plenty of plant food for them all to eat—ferns, conifers, and other kinds of plants that we would not recognize; although there was no grass growing then. If the herds were large they probably had to move along all the time to find new plant food.

Maiasaura would probably have lived for 20 years or more, but as it got older it would have become weak. When the herd moved off to find new food the old *Maiasaura* might have been unable to keep up, and so would have died, perhaps by a river.

3 The First Dinosaurs

The first dinosaurs lived 220 million years ago in the Triassic period. One type of early dinosaur was found in several parts of North America—in the east and in the west. It was called *Coelophysis*. In 1947, a mass of a hundred or more *Coelophysis* skeletons was found at Ghost Ranch, New Mexico. They were dug up by a large team of American scientists.

The skeletons that were dug up included both the large skeletons of adults and the small skeletons of the young. This tells us that it was a large herd that had all been killed at the same time.

We guess that the herd wandered into a boggy area and they could not get out. They all died in the mud and were buried quickly by more mud, which kept the skeletons together and stopped the bones from breaking up. Over the years, the mud hardened into rock and the bones became fossils.

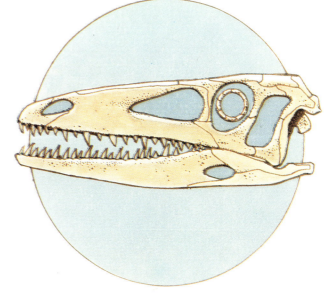

Coelophysis was a meat eater, and probably ate lizards and insects. Some of the specimens from Ghost Ranch actually had small skeletons just where their stomachs were, so we can see what they had eaten just before they died. Some of these small skeletons were baby *Coelophysis*, so it seems possible that the adults were cannibals, and ate their own young!

Coelophysis was from 1 to 3 metres long, but that included a very long tail and a long neck. It would probably have been just shorter than a human adult when it stood up. It ran about on its hind legs and used its arms to grab things just as we do.

Coelophysis had a long head with strong jaws and sharp teeth. In the diagram of its skull (left) you can see its teeth, the eye (near the back) and the nostrils (right at the front).

(4) Growing Bigger

The first really big dinosaur was *Plateosaurus*, which lived at about the same time as *Coelophysis*. You can see how big *Plateosaurus* was compared to *Coelophysis* in the diagram on the right. An adult *Plateosaurus* would have been 8 metres long—about the length of three small cars parked nose to tail. Although *Coelophysis* was a meat eater, it obviously would not have been much of a threat to *Plateosaurus*!

   Plateosaurus was a plant eater. It could have fed on both low bushes and fairly tall trees. We believe that it stood on all fours, but could stand on its hind legs if it wanted to reach up to get some tasty leaves.

The Search for Food

Plateosaurus has been found in Germany and in France. In some places several skeletons were found together. *Plateosaurus* lived in a land of rivers and ponds, split up by deserts. The weather was generally warm and sometimes an area would dry up. Then the herd might travel for hundreds of kilometres to find more food. At other times, there would be heavy rains and big rivers would suddenly flood. The rush of water must have knocked over some of the herd and buried them.

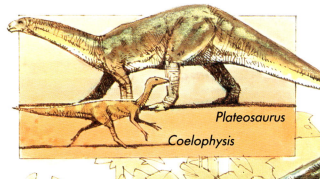

Plateosaurus

Coelophysis

Plateosaurus had a long narrow snout. In the diagram shown above you can see the nostril at the front, and the eye socket second from the back. The teeth are small and leaf-shaped—good for chewing plants.

Next to the skull are the bones of a hand. There is a large hooked thumb which *Plateosaurus* used to drag branches down to its mouth, or to gather up loose leaves from the ground.

Plateosaurus lived in Europe at the end of the Triassic, and it also had relatives living in other countries at that time. For example, the giant *Euskelosaurus* (1) was from 12 to 15 metres long and lived in South Africa. *Massospondylus* (2) was 4 metres long and also lived in South Africa. *Anchisaurus* (3) was only 2 metres long and lived both in South Africa and in North America.

The biggest dinosaur that we know much about is *Brachiosaurus*. This dinosaur was about 23 metres long, and could reach the tops of the tallest trees. If *Brachiosaurus* were to come back today, it could look over the top of a three-storey building. Some people used to think that *Brachiosaurus* stood on the bottom of deep lakes and used its long neck to breathe. However, it has now been shown that it could not have sucked enough air down into its lungs in such deep water.

Brachiosaurus had a low snout with weak peg-like teeth at the front. Its skull was high and the eyes were set well back. *Brachiosaurus* was so huge that it had to eat all day in order to get enough food. It ate leaves from high trees, as well as the lush plants from around lakes. It may also have stood in shallow lakes so that the water could help to support the weight of its massive body.

It now seems possible that *Brachiosaurus* might not have been the biggest dinosaur after all. The bones of a bigger animal, called 'Supersaurus', were found in North America in 1971. *Supersaurus* may have been 30 metres long and from 75 to 100 tonnes in weight.

Then, in 1979, an even bigger dinosaur was found. Known as 'Ultrasaurus', this monster may have also been 30 metres long, and may have weighed 100 to 140 tonnes— the weight of 20 large elephants!

Ultrasaurus

Supersaurus

Brachiosaurus

6 A Day With Diplodocus

Diplodocus was a relative of *Brachiosaurus*, but not so heavy or tall. It had a very long thin neck and tail, however, and was about 4 metres longer than *Brachiosaurus*. Like all dinosaurs, *Diplodocus* slept at night and woke as the sun rose.

During the night, *Diplodocus* probably cooled down and became very slow-moving. It needed the morning sun to warm up and become active. *Diplodocus* fed on leaves. It had long peg-like teeth which were good for stripping leaves off branches.

Diplodocus had to eat all day long just to keep going, and it could not take very big mouthfuls. Although it was a huge animal, it only had a small head, with a mouth not much larger than a cow's mouth. A lakeside was a perfect place for a herd of *Diplodocus*, supplying soft water plants as well as the ferns and bushes on the banks.

At midday, when the sun got very hot, the herd might go right into the water to keep cool. *Diplodocus* was a very long animal, and could probably swim quite well in deep water.

Each *Diplodocus* ate several tonnes of plants each week. A herd of *Diplodocus* could soon eat all the leaves in one place. The trees and bushes would be stripped bare, and there would be nothing left at all. Then the herd would move on.

In the dry season even a small herd of *Diplodocus* could soon run out of food. They had to migrate for long distances to find more food somewhere else. Sometimes, meat-eating dinosaurs would follow, to pick off those that fell behind. But each night, as the sun set, the herd would slow down and eventually stop to sleep.

Stegosaurus is one of the best-known dinosaurs, largely because of its unusual shape. It had a double line of big bony plates running along its back, and four long spikes at the end of its tail. *Stegosaurus* was 9 metres long, and about 5 metres high including the plates. Its head was long and tube-shaped, but its brain was tiny—about the size of a walnut—so it was one of the most stupid of the dinosaurs.

Stegosaurus had only small teeth and it ate plants. It probably could not run very fast and would have made a tempting meal for the larger, meat-eating dinosaurs like *Allosaurus*.

However, the bony plates along its neck and back would have protected *Stegosaurus* from its attacker's dagger-like teeth. Also, by swinging its spiked tail around *Stegosaurus* might manage to wound *Allosaurus* and scare it away.

As well as for protection, we think that *Stegosaurus* used its plates to control its body temperature. The bone of each plate had grooves in it which carried blood vessels. The whole plate was probably covered by skin.

Early in the morning, *Stegosaurus* could stand sideways so that the rays of the sun fell right on the plates and heated its blood. Later, at midday, it could stand with its back to the sun

and let its plates lose some heat.

Stegosaurus lived in North America near the end of the Jurassic period. It was the largest plated dinosaur. Its relatives, *Kentrosaurus*, from East Africa, and *Lexovisaurus*, from England, for example were only 5 metres long. Both had more spikes on their backs, with only a few narrow plates near the front.

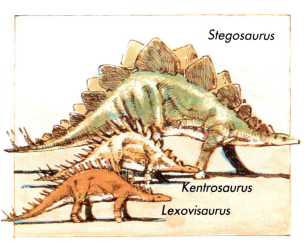

Stegosaurus

Kentrosaurus

Lexovisaurus

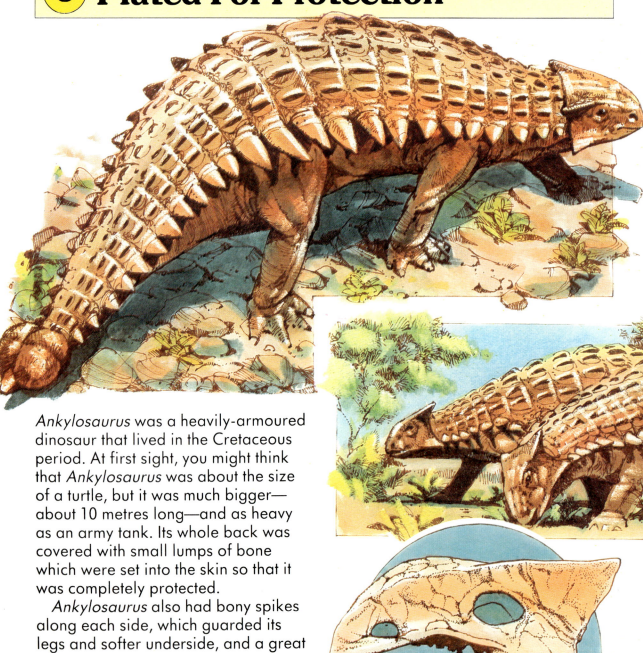

Ankylosaurus was a heavily-armoured dinosaur that lived in the Cretaceous period. At first sight, you might think that *Ankylosaurus* was about the size of a turtle, but it was much bigger— about 10 metres long—and as heavy as an army tank. Its whole back was covered with small lumps of bone which were set into the skin so that it was completely protected.

Ankylosaurus also had bony spikes along each side, which guarded its legs and softer underside, and a great lump of bone at the end of its tail. As if all this was not enough, *Ankylosaurus* had a heavily-protected head. Its skull was completely covered with thick sheets of bone. *Ankylosaurus* was a plant eater, and its teeth were short and blunt.

There was a whole group of 'tank' dinosaurs, most of which lived during the Cretaceous. Two other examples are *Scolosaurus*, which had a pair of spikes on its tail club, and *Hylaeosaurus*, which had no tail club at all, but a good armour of spines on its back. Both were about half the size of *Ankylosaurus*.

During the day, herds of *Ankylosaurus* fed on shrubs and the low branches of trees. At times, a meat eater might come on the scene, such as the powerful *Daspletosaurus*.

Daspletosaurus might try to rip at the flesh of *Ankylosaurus* with its sharp claws, but it would not get through the thick, protective armour. *Ankylosaurus* would crouch down and swing its heavy clubbed tail to try to drive *Daspletosaurus* away.

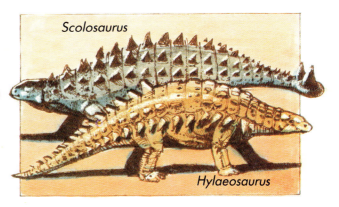
Scolosaurus
Hylaeosaurus

9 Armed With Horns

Triceratops was a horned dinosaur, about 9 metres long. It was a plant eater, like all the other armoured dinosaurs. It grabbed tasty leaves and ferns in its jaws and used its bony beak to chop them off.

Triceratops had a sharp horn on its nose, like a rhinoceros, and two longer horns above its eyes. If a herd was threatened by a meat eater, such as *Albertosaurus*, the young were protected in the middle of the herd.

Protoceratops

Torosaurus

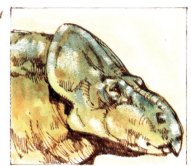

Microceratops

Styracosaurus

Monoclonius

Pachyrhinosaurus

The adult *Triceratops* would form a ring around their young and face outwards. If *Albertosaurus* attacked, the older animals would lower their heads and charge at it with their horns. A charging *Triceratops* with its head down would have had the power of a big truck, and could have seriously wounded any other dinosaur.

At the top of this page you can see some relatives of *Triceratops*. All of these dinosaurs lived in North America during late Cretaceous times, except *Protoceratops* which lived in Mongolia, in Asia. You can see that each of these dinosaurs had a beaked mouth and a large bony frill which protected the weak spot at the back of its neck. Some of them had different arrangements of horns, and others had just bony knobs.

21

Struthiomimus was one of the fastest and cleverest dinosaurs. It was very lightly built, with long powerful legs and a long neck. It is not surprising that it is called the 'ostrich dinosaur'.

Struthiomimus lived in the late Cretaceous period in North America, at the same time as *Ankylosaurus* and *Triceratops*. *Struthiomimus* was 3.5 metres long and was probably as tall as an adult human. The skull of *Struthiomimus* is rather strange. It is very light, with an enormous eye socket. But the oddest thing is that there are no teeth—just bony jaw edges, and yet we think that it was a meat eater.

With such large eye sockets, *Struthiomimus* could obviously see well. It also had a large brain (for a dinosaur, that is) and must have been quicker-witted than many other dinosaurs, like *Stegosaurus* for example.

Struthiomimus had bird-like feet with three toes, each ending in a claw, and strong clawed hands. Its agile hands and long arms would have been useful for digging up roots to eat, or even for digging up eggs from other dinosaurs' nests. It could have gathered up the food in its arms and carried it off to eat in safety from other dinosaurs. We think that it also chased after and ate the small hairy mammals that were present in Cretaceous times.

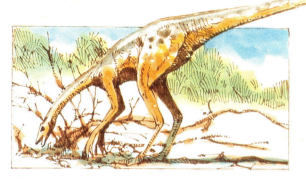

Struthiomimus ran very fast, possibly as fast as a race horse. It probably ran in a very similar way to an ostrich, today. *Struthiomimus* held its long tail out straight behind it to balance its body as it ran.

Deinonychus

Saurornithoides   Compsognathus

Other relatives of *Struthiomimus* were *Deinonychus* (left) which had a huge fierce claw on its foot, *Saurornithoides*, and *Compsognathus* (the smallest dinosaur—smaller than a chicken!)

The 'helmet-heads' were a group of plant-eating dinosaurs that lived in the late Cretaceous. They are also called hadrosaurs, or 'duck-billed dinosaurs' because of their wide duck-like mouths. One of the best known of the duck-bills is *Corythosaurus*, which was about 10 metres long. Like its relatives, it lived in and around lakes, where there was plenty of soft plant food.

The helmet-heads lived in North America and in Mongolia in Asia, and the different species are told apart by the shape of their helmets (right). Some had tall 'spines' pointing backwards or forwards, others a bony lump shaped like a dinner plate or a square sheet. Some had no helmet at all, or else just a small backwards-pointing spike.

Parasaurolophus

Tsintaosaurus

Hypacrosaurus

Lambeosaurus

Edmontosaurus

Saurolophus

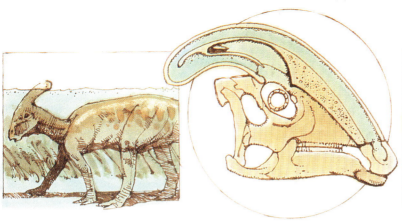

It was thought that the helmet of *Parasaurolophus* was a kind of breathing tube, for use under water.

However, its skull shows that the 'spine' had no air hole. Instead, a long tube ran from the nostril back to the mouth.

All of the duck-bills' helmets were connected to their nostrils and mouths. We believe now that the tube inside the helmet is like the tube in a trumpet. If a helmet-head blew out through its nose, it would make a loud honking noise.

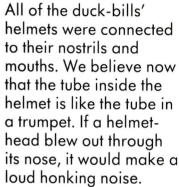

Each different species had a different helmet, so it would have made a different note. These sounds may have been used to help each species to recognize other members of its group.

The duck-bills were very common, and they may have lived on land as well as in lakes. Some skeletons have been found with pine needles in the stomach, so we know what they ate. They could feed on trees on land, or on water plants around the lakes. Duck-bills were good swimmers—and they may even have had webbed feet.

Tyrannosaurus rex may be the most famous dinosaur of all. It was certainly the most deadly. It was 15 metres long and up to 6 metres high. If it came back today, you would not even reach its knee.

Tyrannosaurus had huge curved sharp teeth, each up to 18 cm long— the size of a large steak knife. Each tooth had a jagged edge, too.

Tyrannosaurus lived at the same time as the helmet-heads. A browsing herd of *Parasaurolophus*, for example, would seem to be an easy target. However, although *Tyrannosaurus* was fierce it was not very fast, and all but the oldest and slowest animals would have been able to escape.

Some people think that *Tyrannosaurus* may not even have killed all the animals it ate. It might have fed on the dead bodies of dinosaurs that had been killed accidentally. It would easily have been able to scare off any other smaller scavengers such as *Dromaeosaurus*.

A surprising thing about *Tyrannosaurus* was how small and weak its arms were. It could not even reach its mouth with them, so they were not used in feeding. One idea is that it used them to push itself off the ground when it got up.

One of the more unusual relatives of *Tyrannosaurus* was *Spinosaurus* from North Africa. *Spinosaurus* had a high spiny crest along its back. This may have been to control its body temperature, just as *Stegosaurus* used its plates.

A smaller relative of *Tyrannosaurus* was *Daspletosaurus*, which lived in North America. *Daspletosaurus* was smaller and lighter than *Tyrannosaurus*. It was 'only' 8.5 metres long, but it still had powerful claws and teeth.

13 The First Famous Dinosaur

The first dinosaur to become well known was *Iguanodon*. In 1821, Mrs Mary Mantell was walking along a Sussex lane in England, when she spotted some large fossil teeth in a piece of stone.

She showed them to her husband, Dr Gideon Mantell, who did not know what they were. Only after some years of study, did he decide that the teeth came from a 'giant lizard'.

The Mantells were very interested in the geology of Sussex, and they asked quarry workers to look for more bones. They soon found some more parts of giant skeletons.

Dr Mantell decided to announce these new finds to the leading scientists of his day. In 1825, he held a meeting at the Royal Society in London, and he named the animal *Iguanodon*.

More skeletons of *Iguanodon* were found, and in 1853, Sir Richard Owen had a life-sized model of the whole animal made—it looked like a rhinoceros! A dinner was held inside the model to celebrate.

It soon became obvious, however, that *Iguanodon* usually stood on its hind legs. In 1877 and 1878, a whole herd of *Iguanodon* was found in a coal mine in Belgium, and the skeletons were put on display in Brussels.

Today, we know a lot more about *Iguanodon*. For example, the bone that Richard Owen had thought was a horn on its nose, was actually its long spiky thumb!

Iguanodon was a plant eater, and fed on the leaves of trees. It would have used its spiked thumb to hook the branches towards it, while its long tongue pulled bunches of leaves into its mouth—just as cows gather up grass. It would then have snapped the leaves off with the horny beak at the front of its mouth.

Iguanodon may also have used its spiked thumbs to fight off attacking meat eaters. It could escape from attackers by running away on its hind legs, with its tail stretched out straight behind to balance it.

Iguanodon was about 9 metres long and large herds lived in Europe in the early Cretaceous period.

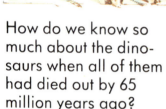

How do we know so much about the dinosaurs when all of them had died out by 65 million years ago?

When a dinosaur died its flesh might have been eaten by various scavengers, until only the bones were left. If the body lay near a river or a lake, it might become buried under sand and mud. Over the years, the sand and mud would harden into rock and the skeleton would become a fossil.

After a great number of years, the rocks might be pushed to the surface, and a fossil collector might spot them. To see the bones clearly the collector would first have to clear away the surrounding rock.

The bones might be delicate, so the collector has to be careful. Fine needles and brushes are used to clean the fossils to avoid any damage.

Then the collector covers the bones with cloths soaked in plaster. This sets hard and protects the bones so they can be sent to a museum.

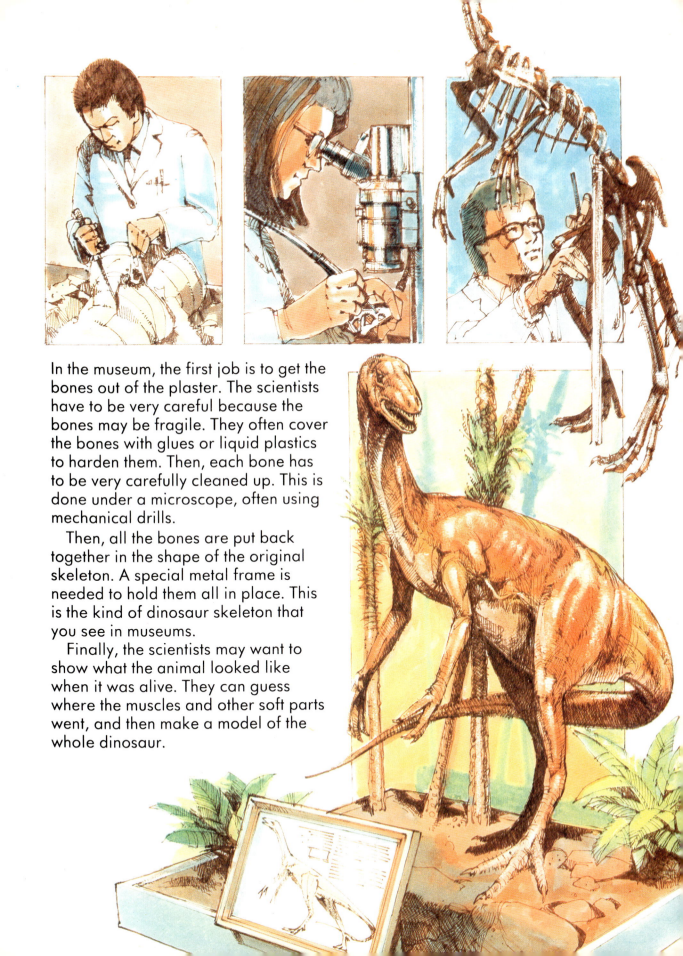

In the museum, the first job is to get the bones out of the plaster. The scientists have to be very careful because the bones may be fragile. They often cover the bones with glues or liquid plastics to harden them. Then, each bone has to be very carefully cleaned up. This is done under a microscope, often using mechanical drills.

Then, all the bones are put back together in the shape of the original skeleton. A special metal frame is needed to hold them all in place. This is the kind of dinosaur skeleton that you see in museums.

Finally, the scientists may want to show what the animal looked like when it was alive. They can guess where the muscles and other soft parts went, and then make a model of the whole dinosaur.

Index

A pronunciation guide is given in brackets after each dinosaur's name.